KIWI
SPEAK

RANDOM HOUSE

UK | USA | Canada | Ireland | Australia
India | New Zealand | South Africa | China

Random House is an imprint of the Penguin Random House group of companies,
whose addresses can be found at global.penguinrandomhouse.com.

First published by Random House New Zealand, 2008
This updated edition published by Penguin Random House New Zealand, 2018

5 7 9 10 8 6 4

Text © Justin Brown, 2018

The moral right of the author has been asserted.

Cover and text design by Rachel Clark © Penguin Random House New Zealand
Typesetting by Kate Barraclough © Penguin Random House New Zealand
Prepress by Image Centre Group
Printed and bound in China by RR Donnelley Asia Printing Solutions Ltd

A catalogue record for this book is available from the National Library of New Zealand.

ISBN 978-0-14-377223-1

penguin.co.nz

KIWI SPEAK

JUSTIN BROWN

RANDOM HOUSE
NEW ZEALAND

Contents

Introduction

New Zealand was the first country to give women the vote. It's also the only place on Earth where builders eat pie sandwiches for lunch. This land of plenty invented the jet boat, spreadable butter and the electric fence. It's also the only place where jandals and shorts are considered 'semi-formal'. This is the home of tiny bathroom basins and 20 million traffic cones, where courgettes are zucchinis, flannels are face cloths, cling film is Glad Wrap, a dairy is a shop, swimming shorts are togs, sweets are lollies, and where homes are insulated by a solitary heated towel rail.

Welcome to *Kiwi Speak*, a book that toasts the way New Zealanders yarn. It celebrates the vowel-flatteners and noun-nasalers among us. There are sayings we used to say and sayings we shouldn't. There are put-downs, pick-me-ups and things you can yell in the pub. You'll discover how Kiwis lose their rag on the road, in the bach and up over the backblocks. The little toerags have their own lingo too. (When they're not wagging, that is. Or is that bunking?)

Maybe you're new to New Zealand. Maybe it fits like an old pair of Stubbies. Whatever the reason, why not pull on your ugg boots, jump in the La-Z-Boy, grab an L&P and check out a few of these beauties. And don't sweat it if you're not a big reader — you'll knock this bastard off in no time. PS: Though these sayings aren't all exclusive to New Zealand, they are used in everyday speech, often having been passed down through generations. Some youngsters born after Helen Clark started running the joint won't know some of the old ones. Conversely, your nana probably reckons the 'Street Speak' section sounds as ludicrous as fart tax. One thing's for sure: New Zealanders, we're different.

So let's have a shandy and celebrate.

CLASSIC
KIWI
SPEAK

From the dairy to the beach to the hangi — in fact, anywhere Kiwis hang out — you'll find the following crackers being used. If you're from out of town, however, and you want to make them sound real authentic, do as most Kiwis do: drop a few vowels here and there, and raise the intonation at the end of each word as if you're asking a question.

A few examples: 'A-medgen' (as in the title of the John Lennon song) going straight to 'bid' (what you sleep on) after scoffing all those 'fush and chups' (shark 'n' tatties). Put it this way — if Dr Seuss was a Kiwi his most famous book would be titled *The Cet in the Het*.

In any case, before we get too carried away and go arse over tit, grab your cuz and have a gawk at the grouse words of wisdom that follow. You'll have it sussed in no time, hunky-dory, sweet as, home 'n' hosed. Righto?

As we say around here, 'Kick it in the guts, Trev!'

'How ya garn?'

Kiwis are right into shortening things: jail terms and odds on Bledisloe Cup matches spring to mind. Alas, it's no different with words. After all, why waste your time with 'Good day, fine sir, how would you be going on this splendiferous morning?' when you could simply get away with the above?

'Good as gold.'

As in: 'How's the job?' 'Good as gold.'

Meaning the employment in question is as good as having gold in your pocket. In the old days, having gold, as opposed to paper money, meant you could exchange it for goods and services anywhere.

'Ka pai!'

Maori for 'good'. Even your average Palagi, or Honky, feels confident enough using the above. Indeed, some — the daring and reckless Pakeha — even attempt to place it in a full sentence: 'Ka pai kai (food) in my puku (belly).'

'Haven't seen you in yonks!'

A cracker of a word, yonks. Literally meaning 'ages', one theory is that it comes from donkey's years. Another is that it's taken from years, months and weeks.

'She'll be right!'

Arguably the most popular Kiwi phrase of all time. Can be used in response to a number of enquiries: 'Shall we lock the car?'; 'Do we have enough petrol to get us to Blenheim?'; 'Are you wearing a condom?'

'You can't handle the jandal!'

I only recently learnt that the common Kiwi jandal got its name from a contraction of 'Japanese sandal'. The above would have been perfect in a New Zealand version of *A Few Good Men*: 'You can't handle . . . the jandal!'

'He's a kumara short of a hangi.'

The lights are on but nobody's home. His elevator doesn't go to the top. Dumber than a box of rocks. Not playing with a full deck. If you don't get my drift by now, you obviously don't have both oars in the water.

'Ya reckon?'

Typical response to your best friend's admission to having the hots for the guy from accounts who everyone else thinks is a complete bogan.

'Bring a plate.'

Many a newbie to these shores has stubbed their toe on this one. Despite the instruction, this does not mean 'We're short of plates so please bring one', but rather, 'Bring a plate with something delicious on it. And don't forget to take it home. We've got enough plates.'

'Sweet as.'

As Kiwi as a potato-top pie, a box of Jaffas or a game of Swingball. Literally translates to 'yes', or 'agreed'. 'F***ing A' or 'Right as rain' can also be used.

'Average as.'

Complete opposite of the above.

'I'm going to see a man about a dog.'

More often than not, this saying comes out of the Kiwi male's mouth. And it has many meanings: 'I'm going trout fishing'; 'The pokies are calling my name'; 'Must get that boat I've always promised myself'.

'Yeah . . . nah.'

Likely response from a New Zealand sports captain when being interviewed post-match, as in: 'Yeah . . . nah, the game was ours for the taking but we just couldn't put the final nail in the coffin.' 'So does this mean retirement for you as captain?' 'Yeah . . . nah . . . yeah . . . nah.' Clear as mud.

'She's a bit of a dag.'

The woman in question, who has come to a Kiwi-themed party dressed as Peter Plumley-Walker (true story), is a bit of a 'hard case', comedian or joker. (Plumley-Walker was a cricket umpire who famously died during a bondage and discipline session in 1989 and whose still-bound body was turfed over the Huka Falls.)

'No wucking furries.'

A classic piece of Kiwi Speak that can even be used in front of a toddler. Not dissimilar to the well-worn term 'She had a cunning array of stunts.'

'Piece of piss, mate.'

See above.

'Good on ya.'

Not a good one to send by text as it can be taken two ways. 'Good on ya', as in, 'I'm stoked for you, good job'. Alternatively, 'Oh, good on ya', as in, 'Thanks for spilling Coke all over my new boardies!'

'GO-ORNE, be a sport!'

Used by the bludger who's doing his best to scrounge your last potato fritter.

'Geez, I busted a gut.'

To make an intense effort by mowing the lawn, trimming the hedges and cleaning the gutters. Normally, it must be said, because you stumbled in at 4am and slept in your mother-in-law's bathroom.

'Chooooice!'

A call heard from one side of London to the other when a parcel containing Wattie's tomato sauce, Pineapple Lumps, Jaffas and Marmite is ripped open. And hidden from every other bludging dosser.

'What are ya?'

A Kiwi's way of saying, 'Is that all you've got?'

The most effective reply, as I discovered in primary school, is 'What are *you*?'

'He's on a cushy number.'

The employee in question works four-hour days, gets a company car, overseas trips, an expense account, client lunches and front-row seats to big gigs. Yes, the person in question *is* hated — but by God they're happy!

'She's built like a brick shithouse.'

A good Kiwi to have on your side should you be on the receiving end of a knuckle sandwich.

'It was a bloody mish all right!'

In other words: 'My three-year-old could have given better directions!' ('Mish' being short for 'mission'.)

'Up at sparrow's fart, gotta drive to Parther's Arse.'

When Kiwi kids find out they're allowed to say 'Whakapapa' without getting into trouble, they think all their Christmases have come at once. One good thing about being an adult, apart from being allowed to stay up to watch the entire LOTR trilogy, is calling the place name Arthur's Pass the above.

'Bring round half a doz and we'll make a night of it.'

The best parties are unplanned, which explains why so many people are let down on New Year's Eve. The six beers, as mentioned above, won't exactly set the world on fire, but when a Kiwi says 'make a night of it' you may as well pack the PS4 and leave the car at home.

'They'll charge you an arm and a leg.'

Buying Bluff oysters in Auckland is not for the faint-hearted. Indeed, chucking in the job, moving to Southland and setting up a fishing charter would be far more affordable. Not to mention fun.

'Where's the dunny?'

Translation: 'Could you show me the way to the washroom, please?'

Other Kiwi names for the little boys' room: 'long drop', 'bog', 'shitter', 'lav' and 'loo'.

'What's for pud?'

Translation: 'Will there be a sweet treat following the main course?'

Response: 'Yeah, if you get up and make it!'

'Spot on!'

Absolutely correct. Exactly right. 100 per cent.
Inspired a kids' TV show of the same name.

'Rough as guts.'

This Kiwi isn't averse to getting his hands dirty or afraid of a little bit of hard work. Alternatively, it can mean the New Zealander in question fell out of the ugly tree and hit every branch on the way down. You get the idea.

'Can't come in, boss. Got the dreaded lurgy.'

There's a fine art to throwing a sickie, though telling all and sundry that you have the Zika virus or Ebola will normally do it. The above is slang for something less serious but more catching. Not to mention honest!

'Righto, give it heaps!'

Typically muttered to your best mate who has bought, against everyone's advice, the worst car in the country. Alas, the next couple of minutes won't be pretty; best to block the kids' ears unless you want them to hear the epitome of profanity.

'Wrap your laughing gear around that one.'

First mastered by the irreverent Barry Crump who, when not driving poor old Scotty to drink in the Toyota ads in the 1980s, was taking his ute up tracks only bovines should use.

'Up shit creek in leaky gumboots.' 'Up the boohai shooting pukekos with a popgun.'

Whenever the New Zealand cricket team play a test against Australia, they inevitably lose more wickets than they make runs. The above sayings should cover how the average fan feels knowing the five-day match will be finished in two.

'I wasn't born yesterday.'

Likely reply to: 'I heard they took the word "gullible" out of the dictionary.' Even more colloquial is the sarcastic yet extremely effective 'Yeah right!'

'Just yanking your chain.'

'I'm pulling your leg! The All Blacks didn't *really* lose the quarter-final against France. But don't watch the replay, it's boring . . . hey, look over there!'

'Helengrad.'

Politicians crave being talked about. A greater honour is being given a nickname that demonstrates your so-called iron grip of the nation. To some, Helen Clark's Wellington was known as Helengrad during her three terms as PM.

'Wellywood.'

Another nickname for the capital, this time given to Weta Workshop and Weta Digital for bringing Hollywood's typical duties downunder. It also meant a shorter commute for Peter Jackson.

'Waikikamukau.'

Before most Kiwis learnt how to pronounce Maori names properly — and some sports commentators still make a dog's breakfast of it — the above fictional town was, and is, still known as Why Kick a Moo Cow. While we're on questionable humour, White Homo (Waitomo) and Land of the Wrong White Crowd would have to make the cut too.

'Tu meke.'

'Too much.' In a more formal sense, tu meke translates to 'astonishing'.

'Ngati Pakeha.'

Prefix used in Maori tribal names, as in Ngati Porou, but applied to the white fullahs. Mount Egganaki, a combo of Mt Egmont and Mt Taranaki, works on the same principle.

'Check out his puku.'

Puku refers to said food connoisseur's stomach, which resembles a Swiss ball due to pigging out on too much kai (food).

'Half pai/half pie.'

Part English/part Maori. Derived from 'half-baked'. As in:
'Don't do it half pai (half good), do it properly. Egg.'

'Tutu.'

Not to be confused with a ballet dress of the same name, to tutu
means to fiddle or tinker with something. As in: 'I'm just going to
the shed to have a bit of a tutu with my rocket launcher.'

'Munted.'

Sadly, this term was best used to describe the devastation following the 2011
Christchurch earthquake. In the early hours after the quake, the then mayor
Bob Parker was asked how things were, to which he replied, 'It's munted.'

MUM
SPEAK

Kiwi mums are a wonderful breed. They're smart, spunky and possess a don't-mess-with-me attitude. They're magicians, too, able to produce an unending supply of Pineapple Lumps and lemonade Popsicles should the need arise. (Or if they need to make a really good bribe.) And despite being knackered from a day's work, they still find the time to make Marmite on toast and hot Milo when you return from school.

The Kiwi mum is there when your bunny dies. She watches *Stranger Things* even though she'd rather be watching *The Good Wife*. She is the Queen of Feigning Enthusiasm when, in reality, she'd much prefer a glass of wine and a chat on the phone (uninterrupted).

'It's puckarooed!'

The dishwasher in question is buggered, stuffed or — another classic Kiwi term — completely had it. Puckarooed is actually a corruption of the Maori word 'pakaru', meaning 'broken' or 'ruined'. Either way, it won't change the fact that the only decision you'll be making in the next five minutes is whether you'll be washing or drying.

'Do you want a clip around the ear?'

Normally uttered when the said Kiwi mum has discovered cigarettes in her child's school bag.

'If everyone else jumped off the Harbour Bridge, would you?'

An adventurous Kiwi kid is surely the wrong person to ask, 'If everyone else jumped in the Waitemata, would you?' 'Hell, yeah, what time?'

'What's the magic word?'

Every family has their own magic word — 'please', 'abracadabra' and 'hocus pocus' seem to do the trick — though there are a few Kiwi kids who take their cue from the *The Addams Family* movies: 'What's the magic word?' 'NOW!'

'Don't pea on the table.'

I'm guilty of dad jokes myself. The above was my mother's Achilles heel, always used when the said lone vegetable rolled next to the bowl of mashed spuds.

'Shall I put the "spew-mante" in the fridge?'

Back in the day, Kiwi mums liked a bottle of Bernadino because it was cheap. Kiwi teens prefer cask wine because once it's finished the plastic bladder makes a fantastic football. Miami Wine Cooler used to cop a fair bit of flak but Spumante (pronounced 'spew-mante') was, for the obvious reasons, easily the most memorable.

'If you're good, you can have a Jelly Tip.'

Kiwi kids don't realise there is nothing better (and never will be) than standing on the back lawn, naked, eating chocolate-covered ice cream and jelly on a stick. That's life, right there.

Note: Recently my daughter asked me why the ice cream in question isn't a Jelly *Bottom*? Her thinking being, when you eat a Jelly Tip the good times are over as soon as you bite into it. If the jelly was at the bottom there would be something to look forward to. Your move, Tip Top.

'Marjorie and Bruce are going to the bach for Waitangi Day.'

You wouldn't hear this sentence anywhere else on the planet. A bach (Kiwi for beach house) is the ultimate retreat on New Zealand's national day, in the balmy month of February.

'No wonder you're not hungry, you had a 50c mix half an hour ago!'

Once upon a time a bag of lollies was the size of your hand. They lasted for weeks. And you could never eat all your tea. Oh well . . .

'Sharon's moving to the wop-wops.'

Otherwise known as the 'boonies', the wop-wops are literally the back of beyond: no broadband; no neighbours; no cops. (You didn't hear that last bit from me.)

'A boy in Whanganui had his eye out with a rubber band.'

Regardless of the dangerous activity, the boy in Whanganui with the bad aim was always used as an example. Alas, it never worked, with most kids willing to lose a body part if it meant they could maim their sibling.

'Any more backchat and you won't be going to the blue-light disco.'

The blue-light disco was a dance put on by the police. It was a place where 12-year-old boys wished they could hug the girls when they danced, instead of the walls. Hormones, testosterone, Fanta and Dad (who parked 28 blocks away).

'Wait till your father gets home.'

You have to feel for the dad who works all day, endures a heinous traffic jam and is dying for a beer, only to find once he walks in the front door that he has to yell at his kid for feeding crayons to the family axolotl.

'Say ta?'

It would be fine if this was said just the once. Sadly, for first-time parents anyway, it's monotony epitomised: 'Ta? Ta? Ta? Callum, say ta? Ta? Ta? Ta? Callum! Ta! Ta!' This drawn-out manners lesson is typically followed by 'Where have our guests gone?'

'If you eat that now, you'll ruin your dinner.'

The above is likely to be followed with the classic, clichéd, downright obvious, 'When they're gone, they're gone!'

'Not tonight, love, I'm had it.'

Bad news for Dad.

'Who won?'

This is normally asked by the Kiwi wife, who had the common sense to go to bed four hours before her sports-mad husband. The surly response is always the same: 'THEM!', which is typically followed by 'It's *always* them!'

'Heh, heh, one day you'll be prime minister!'

My mum, I'm sure like many others across New Zealand, used to tug on my cheeks while saying the above. Former PM Robert Muldoon had this dent in his face, the joke being that if Mum pulled mine long enough, I may one day get to run the country. And ruin it, like Muldoon. That aside, he did have the best comebacks. When a journalist once hassled him for kicking a man when he was down, 'Piggy' replied, 'When better? Heh, heh, heh!'

'Hercules Morse as big as a horse, Muffin McLay like a bundle of hay . . .'

'. . . and Hairy Maclary from Donaldson's Dairy.' There wouldn't be many young Kiwi mums who haven't read these lines to their toddlers in bed.

'Who spilt pav on my Edmonds cookbook?'

Hot debate continues to rage on who invented the pavlova, the strongest contenders, of course, being our trans-Tasman neighbours. But Australia stole Phar Lap, Crowded House and Russell Crowe. We keep the pav!

Note: As for the cookbook, it's one of the biggest-selling New Zealand books of all time, constantly on the bestseller lists.

'Slip, slop, slap before you go anywhere, mister!'

A health campaign in New Zealand that asked folk to 'Slip on a shirt, slop on sunscreen and slap on a hat' to prevent skin cancer.

DAD
SPEAK

New Zealand dads are one of a kind. The good ones are out there on Saturday mornings taking their kids to sport. The bad ones are still wearing Stubbies. Most Kiwi dads have time for the family, as long as that means having 80 minutes off to watch the rugby. They're proud of their sheds and very protective of their barbecues, not to mention their daughters. They're pedantic at packing the boot on holidays and, once there, are always the first to challenge you at Swingball.

Much like Kiwi mums, dads have a unique way of talking. (Of course, sometimes it takes little more than a look to realise you're in hot water.) For many of these sayings, you have your grandfather to blame. Or your great-grandfather. And, before you blokes criticise, just remember that when you become a pedantic packer and Stubbies model you too will be belting them out with reckless abandon.

'Go and ask your mother.'

The inevitable reply: 'I've already asked her — she said no.'

'Go and ask your mother for a plate for the meat.'

If I had a sausage for every time I heard my dad say this, I'd have the world's biggest casserole. As we all know, you're not to put cooked meat on the plate you brought the raw stuff out on. As a result, dads all over New Zealand request a clean plate upon which to put their culinary — normally 'Cajun' — masterpieces.

'I'm off to the shed, I could be a while.'

It took me a long time to realise why fathers were so in awe of the common garden shed. Now I understand completely. The 'den', 'man-space' or 'cave' is purely an escape from the kids. Example: 'Just going to sweep the shed for the fourth time today, love. By the way, Jack needs a nappy change.'

'Oh, give me a break!'

This is typically heard when the said Kiwi dad's lawnmower has run out of petrol with only a tiny patch of grass left. Or it's muttered when he can't wind that stupid plastic cord onto the inside of the weedeater.

'Get in the car, we're leaving!'

This can be used on a number of occasions:

• when you superglue your sister's hands together;

• when you pop the rellies' waterbed;

• when, upon seeing an obese shopper at the supermarket checkout, you say, 'Wow, that man has a baby in his tummy!'

'Keep these grades up and you'll be a third-year fifth!'

Being 'held back' in school was embarrassing to a class pet. To a delinquent it was an honour. (2018 equivalent — repeating Year 11 for the third time.)

'Where's your stack hat?'

Also known as a 'skid lid', bicycle helmets were made compulsory on New Zealand roads in 1994. Our parents have no idea how lucky they were, never having to wear one.

'Okay, I've got four fish, three potato fritters, one chip and one spring roll.'

What Kiwi dad didn't stand in the lounge with a scrap of paper and a pen taking orders on a Friday night? If you were lucky he'd even take you to the fish and chip shop, where you waited with bated breath for 'number 54'.

'I'm gonna hit the hay, gotta be up for the dawn parade.'

The dawn parade is the most popular observance of Anzac Day, timed to represent the initial landings at Gallipoli on 25 April 1915. The time is also poignant for veterans who recall the routine dawn 'stand-to' of their war service. It's an emotional experience and one that every Kiwi youngster should get out of bed for.

'One more over, then I'll come up to bed.'

An over in cricket is roughly three minutes long, and that's where most Kiwi cricket fans lose the concept of time. One over becomes two, becomes midnight, becomes grumpy Dad come sunrise. It's best to remember that New Zealand teams mostly win when we're asleep.

'I've only got enough time for an Aussie shower.'

Muttered when the said Kiwi dad has been chopping bamboo all afternoon and doesn't have time for a shit, shower and shave before going out for tea. Thank God for Brut 33 and Old Spice.

'Did you shit the bed?'

The only reason to be up at sparrow's fart is to watch a fellow Kiwi compete for an Olympic gold medal on the other side of the world. A more literal explanation may be directly related to the saying itself, which sadly happens very early, or very late, in life.

'She went mad so I shot her.'

A Kiwi dad's response to the overused, not to mention
downright annoying, 'Where's Mum?'

'Wait till your mother gets home!'

See similar entry in Mum Speak.

'I could make that.'

Kiwi dads are a resourceful bunch. Indeed, if one sees an elaborate piece of art made out of nothing but chicken wire, garden rakes and pantyhose, he drives home straight away to make it.

'If you clean your rugby boots you can have a Hundreds and Thousands sandwich.'

Otherwise known as 'fairy bread' (though not to boys!), you can't beat Hundreds and Thousands on fresh white bread with butter. Almost worth tidying your room for.

'Bit nippy round the pipis!'

Kiwi Speak for 'She's a bit cold out!' Pipi, a New Zealand shellfish, have no relevance whatsoever to the nether regions — but it does rhyme pretty well, don't you think?

'Do you want me to get the wooden spoon?'

An intelligent ratbag would undoubtedly say no. Sadly, however, most kids stand there waiting for another option.

'Had a fight with the lawnmower, mate?'

Unfortunately, some men always walk out of the barber's looking like Forrest Gump.

'You can watch *The Block*, but as soon as the ABs start we're switching over.'

For the Kiwi dad, nothing is more sacred than watching his beloved All Blacks. Fans have been known to duck out of funerals and delay weddings to watch them.

Note: Not a good time (as my mother knows) to dust the TV screen.

'Get your A into G, you little toerag!'

The 'A' is otherwise known as your butt. The 'G' means 'gear'. Even though this sounds like a telling-off, toerag is actually a term of endearment. The definition derives from old England, where convicts once tied bits of shirt around their toes and feet as makeshift socks, hence 'toerag' means scoundrel, criminal or thief.

'Go and get me some ciggies from the dairy. I'll time ya.'

Extremely unlikely to be used nowadays, as you have to be 18 to buy smokes, but heard regularly when I was a nipper. Especially tempting when there was a Buzz Bar or Toffee Milk up for grabs.

'Sure, go for a swim, but if you drown, don't come crying to me!'

Luckily, Kiwi kids, like every ankle-biter on the planet, have never understood sarcasm.

'Go and play in the traffic.'

'You're away with the fairies!'

'No Netflix on a school night!'

'No need to pack a sad.'

NANA
SPEAK

Don't be fooled by their age — Kiwi grandmas and grandads know exactly what's going on. Call them pop, call them nana — just don't call them late for breakfast. They don't miss a trick either, and have more sayings than you've had hot dinners. Many Kiwi 'nana-isms' are a hangover from the British days.

'TTFN!'

Short for 'Ta-ta for now', although, much like the way 'Jack' is supposed to be short for 'John', it doesn't seem to save time for anyone.

'Toodle-pip.'

An old-fashioned way of saying 'Spot you later'.

'Let's have some hymn hums.'

Nana Speak for a music jam (with piano, guitars and comb and paper).

'Be back in two ticks, just going for a tinkle.'

Wouldn't you prefer hearing the above over 'Going for a slash'?

'Just going for a wizz, won't be a jiffy. Back in two shakes of a lamb's tail.'

See above.

'Gordon Bennett! Who left my wireless out in the rain?'

There are many origins for the above, but there's no doubt the British comedies *Steptoe and Son* and *Only Fools and Horses* made the saying part of the New Zealand vernacular. As for the wireless? That's Grandad's transistor, which became a Walkman, then an iPod, and now music in 'the cloud' we don't even own.

'You couldn't see the road to the dunny if it had red flags on it!'

'Wherever you be, let your wind go free . . .'

'. . . for trying to hold it in will be the death of ye!' Well, this was true of my nana, anyway. Yours, like many others, may have opted for the alternative: 'Ladies should be polite and not ignite until out of sight.'

'It's the Asian invasion.'

About as un-PC as you can get, but still used by some grandparents. Alas, most people who use this phrase nowadays often pre-empt it with 'Now, I'm not a racist, but . . .'

'Fill the flagon up while you're there.'

Aluminium cans are a grand invention, but nothing beats the solid feel of an empty sherry flagon. There were stories in there, and jokes, and lies. And when it was empty you went and swapped it for a full one!

'Happy as Larry.'

The earliest printed usage of the above is from the New Zealand writer G Meredith, dating from around 1875: 'We would be as happy as Larry if it were not for the rats.'

'Box of fluffies.'

Fluffy ducks are supposed to be cute. And I suppose a whole box of them would make one feel warm and fuzzy. Ironically, the above saying is often used in a sarcastic manner, as in: 'How ya feeling?' 'Box of fluffies.' Translation: 'Pretty shite, actually.' Nana, of course, wouldn't put it quite like that.

'Till the cows come home.'

Many believe this saying originated in 1829. At least, that's when it first appeared in the *London Times*, which ran the following story: 'If the Duke will but do what he unquestionably can do, and propose a Catholic Bill with securities, he may be Minister "until the cows come home".'

'She's gone up north for a while.'

In the old days, people used to brush a lot of stuff under the rug. Isn't it funny that in this case she returned nine months later . . .

'You make a better door than a window.'

After you've shut the door — and stopped whacking your sister with the draught-snake — be sure not to stand in front of the telly while your gran's watching *Antiques Roadshow*.

'Fill 'er up at the bowser.'

Old-school name for the humble petrol pump.

'Were you born in a tent?'

I love the sarcasm in this saying — I can pretty much guarantee my nana knew
I wasn't born in a tent, but she still had the cheek to ask every time I forgot
to close the lounge door. On that note, does anyone use those multicoloured,
home-knitted, ridiculous-looking draught-snakes any more? Thought not.

TV
SPEAK

In the old days, a lot of New Zealand TV ads used to be better than the actual programmes. Maybe that's because we only had two channels. Actually, make that one — Telethon hogged one channel for nearly a week!

Either way, there was definitely less choice on the goggle box. Here are some sayings Kiwis learnt from the bits in between *Top Town* and *Spot On*.

'Relax, you're soaking in it!'

This was a Madgism. Madge was the hands and nails expert from the Palmolive ads. She was a bit of a know-it-all with an acerbic wit, advising women of the wondrous dishwashing liquid 'which softens hands while you do dishes!' Many of those early New Zealand ads came straight out of Australia. Even so, it may surprise some to know that Madge was actually an American actress: Jan Miner, from New York, appeared on and off Broadway from the 1940s to the 1980s. Without a doubt, though, she won most widespread attention as Madge, a character she played for 27 years. Jan Miner died in 2004, aged 86.

'Ee, Ee, Brucie!'

Why we find irritating Aussies so endearing is anyone's guess. (Think Vince Martin.) Maybe Brucie, who I believe was hawking cars, couldn't find any work on *Neighbours* or *The Sullivans*. As for Vince, he's surely a retread by now.

'We are the boys from down on the farm, we really know our cheese!'

Marketing genius. An ad that all Kiwis sang — all thanks to Ches and Dale.

'You can rock it,
you can roll it!
You can lock the rock
and put your feet up.
You can sit right back
and really enjoy
Your genuine La-Z-Boy!'

If you thought Ray Woolf was famous only for this La-Z-Boy ad, think again. Most recently he appeared in *King Kong*. He once hosted his own TV show, starred on *Play School* and appeared on *Shortland Street*.

Note: There are only nine New Zealanders who *haven't* been on *Shortland Street*.

'Go for G, G, G, G, G, G, G, G, Gerard! Go for Gerard and your roof is looking good!'

Everyone remembers annoying jingles. In this case, add New Zealand's version of Engelbert Humperdinck, John Rowles, along with his young family — who just happen to be celebrating their new Gerard roof — and you have a tune that stuck to your brain like superglue. Though, to be honest, I never remember Rowles having such a pronounced stutter.

'You're not in Guatemala now, Dr Ropata.'

As soon as Nurse Carrie Burton uttered this line to Dr Hone Ropata (played by Temuera Morrison) in the premiere episode of New Zealand's longest-running soap, *Shortland Street*, it began life as a popular Kiwi saying.
Example: 'These pies aren't like the ones at my local!'
'You're not in Guatemala now, Dr Ropata.'

'Any . . . last requests?'

Walk up to anyone who hung out in New Zealand in the
'80s and ask this. (Note: The pause is vital.)

A reply will be forthright, a hand expectant: 'Ah, Pixie Caramel.'

'Marrrrrrrrrrrrrrrvelous!'

As echoed by TV One when John Campbell left
the coveted 7pm prime-time slot.

'Two all-beef patties, special sauce, lettuce, cheese, pickles, onions on a sesame-seed bun!'

Once upon a time, when bad food wasn't bad for you, McDonald's
used to say if you could sing the above quickly enough they would
give you a free burger. If only schools had such incentives!

'Tiger, Tiger, Jelly Meat for dinner!'

The cat in question was eating what some Kiwis say used to make up the contents of your average servo pie.

'I'm taking this bloody car to Invercargill, boy!'

From the classic Kiwi road-trip movie *Goodbye Pork Pie* and the consequent spike in sales of yellow Minis.

'Life's a whole long
journey, boy,
before you grow too old,
don't miss the opportunity
to strike a little gold . . .
Have a Crunchie,
hokey pokey bar.
Crazy Crunchie,
hokey pokey bar!'

New Zealand's only train robbery — an advert for the still-popular Crunchie.

'Those were our people today. That's *Holmes* tonight.'

The nightly sign-off by TV host Paul Holmes (RIP). He was on our screens for decades, endured scandals, *Dancing with the Stars* and multiple aircraft crashes. He'll be remembered fondly for calling MP Tariana Turia a 'confused bag of lard', and former United Nations Secretary-General Kofi Annan a 'cheeky darkie' on his radio show.

'Where'd I get my bag?
Lands for Bags, of course!'

Some ads stick, no matter how bad they are. Then along comes some genius who takes the mickey out of it. Case in point — Billy T James: 'Where'd I get my bag? I nicked it, eh!'

'I'll have an "O" for Awesome.'

Little did boxer David Tua know, after making this embarrassing slip on *Wheel of Fortune*, that it would be used colloquially all over the country, not to mention printed on T-shirts and posters. Personally, I think David's right — O for Oarsome is exactly how it should be spelt!

'Who stole the telly? Who stole the telly? Morris was very depressed!'

This was an NZI ad. Script: Cat chases parrot. Parrot gets so excited he knocks a cup off the kitchen sink. Then: 'They've paid! They've paid!' Stunning. Memorable. Or maybe I just remember it that way because I was six.

'If you drink and drive, you're a bloody idiot!'

The follow-up ad, sadly, never made it to the screen: 'Don't drink and drive — you might hit a bump and spill your drink.'

'It's the same day, David.'

Another ad in the drink-driving series. David, lying in bed with a smashed leg, having killed a couple of people in a car accident, is visited by his girlfriend. To rub salt into the wound, she brings in a speeding ticket and relays the news that he was doing 130 km/h minutes before the crash. (Note: 'Not a good time, honey!')

'It's moments like these you need Minties!'

The Minties ad, ruthless in laughing at other people's misfortunes, was a truly memorable piece of television. Now, sadly, we're a little too PC to laugh at rugby players tripping over, or cricketers slipping on the proverbial banana skin.

'So Dad stopped the car, and Hugo said, "You go," but I said, "No, you go!" . . . Thank goodness for Kentucky Fried!'

Ah, the good old days, when they weren't afraid to tell us what the 'F' stood for.

'If it's not right, we'll put it right. And it's the putting right that counts.'

Mail-order specialists LV Martin & Son — 'and you won't be stuck with a lemon'.

'Not even, ow!'

Jeff da Maori's sage words from *bro'Town*, New Zealand's first local prime-time animated TV show.

'That messy trough should be gone-burger by the weekend.'

Like an old pair of jeans, TV One's weather presenter Jim Hickey has been with us through the highs and the lows. He retired and ran a cafe in New Plymouth, then, thankfully, returned to our screens four years later, before finally retiring at the end of 2014.

'Keep cool till *After School*!'

Olly Ohlson was the best thing on TV in the '80s, aside from *The Snorks* and *Inspector Gadget*.

'What's it going to be, Hokitika — the money or the bag?'

Small New Zealand towns came alive, all thanks to Selwyn Toogood and his iconic travelling quiz show *It's in the Bag*.

'Eat some ice creams, do some bombs!'

Google this vid and you'll discover what it felt like to grow up in New Zealand. Minus God. You'll know what I mean when you see it.

'Nek minnit.'

'Left my scooter outside the dairy, nek minnit . . .' Kiwi skateboarder Levi Hawken's video lamenting his broken ride has now had over three million views, and in 2011 was the sixth most searched term in New Zealand on Google.

'I'm beached as!'

Originates from an online video made by a pair of Aussies who mimic the Kiwi accent. The video shows a cartoon of a beached whale who says to a passing bird, 'Oh, no, I'm beached as!' Translation: 'Up the creek without a paddle. I'm screwed. I'm ruined.'

'Naturally, I finished my set.'

Kiwi Cameron Leslie was at a gym near the site of a bombing in Oslo, Norway, in July 2011. Instead of retelling the horror of the situation nearby, he instead told *Campbell Live* about his awesome workout. Leslie later apologised for his joke.

'Always blow on the pie.'

Sometimes governments create slogans to make our lives safer. 'Mind the Gap' on London's Underground comes to mind. In New Zealand, however, not waiting the full 45 minutes before hoeing into a steak and cheese pie can be fatal, as this well-known saying from the TV show *Police Ten 7* demonstrates.

'You know I can't grab your ghost chips!'

A TV ad made to discourage drink-driving, clearly made by someone under the influence.

FARM
SPEAK

Righto, let's get them all out of the way before we begin:

Did you hear the Kiwis have a new use for sheep? Meat and wool.

How do Kiwis find sheep in long grass? Very nice, thank you very much.

A farmer's mate is having his way with a sheep in the barn back of beyond. Upon finding his friend, the farmer yells, 'Hey, you're supposed to be shearing that sheep!' The response? 'You find your own bloody sheep!'

Okay. Can we continue? Good.

With 30 million sheep in New Zealand, the average Kiwi has to know what they're talking about on the farm, even if it means faking it. In this chapter are sayings for townies and cow cockies alike.

PS: Farmers (from anywhere) don't suffer fools gladly. Be sure to say the following in a confident, don't-mess-with-me tone.

PPS: This chapter is dedicated to my incredible Uncle Don and Aunty Margie, who lived on their farm in Mangaweka for over 45 years. Black singlet, two sausages for breakfast, as Kiwi as they come.

'Get in there, ya mongrel!'
'Get in behind!'
'Wayleggo!'

You'll hear the above yelled from paddocks in Pukekohe to the backblocks in Balclutha. It's generally directed at the dog with selective hearing and a wandering mind.

'He's all hat and no horse.'

Refers to the joker who's a talker, not a doer.

'The old Fergie's stuffed.'

On a farm it is common to refer not in general terms to the tractor — or the sheep, or even the woolshed — as a townie might. It's specifically the Fergie (short for tractor make Massey Ferguson) or the steel wheel.

'Poor thing's wool blind.'

The said sheep's wool has literally grown over its eyes.
As a result he doesn't see fences, opting instead to run straight into them.

'Blue's a bit whip-shy. If he doesn't play his cards right, there'll be no tucker.'

Blue is the dog that cowers or hides when the stock whip comes out.
Then again, what dog wouldn't?

'Barry's coming over later. He's an expert bum-barber.'

Crutching is the process of cleaning dags from around a sheep's
bum. And Barry the Bum Barber's the lucky guy to do it!

Note: Would you put that job title on your CV?

'Wish I'd brought my bush nightie, it's colder than a witch's tit.'

It's hard to believe, but farmers get cold too. When the temperature drops — and no one's looking — the said Good Keen Bloke pulls on his extra-long Swannie and puts a brew on.

'He's a real number 8 wire man.'

He's your go-to guy. Sometimes called a Swanndri man, or your Swannie bloke.

'You'll be pearl diving at the dag-pickers' ball if you carry on like that!'

The farming equivalent of time out on the naughty step. The above applies to the farmhand who has been relegated to the woolshed to sort the wool from the dags.

'Rattle your dags!'

Without a doubt the most-used saying on the farm. Epitomised on the TV screen by Fred 'Kick it in the guts, Trev!' Dagg, but still used all over the show as a way to let stock know they need to get a move on. (Note for UK farmers: Dingle berries and dags are the same thing, even if yours sound like something that should go with ice cream.) The above refers to the noise often made by the (dried) dags of scurrying, uncrutched sheep. 'Shake your shirt' (another Kiwi saying) will have a similar effect. (RIP John Clarke aka Fred Dagg. Thanks for the laughs.)

'Piss in your own time!'

This time Blue is taking a leak and admiring the view
when he should be mustering for his master.

'Little bugger's gate-shy!'

For the sheep that, for whatever reason, don't like the look of that gate!
They baulk and hesitate, often needing a boot up the bum for effect.

'Don's taking up the burnt chops.'

Don is not, as you might imagine, scraping the charred remains from
the barbie, but is out mustering, bringing in the wool.

'These hockey sticks are a bit chewy. Must have been a tough old ewe.'

Some farm meat has the texture of bubblegum. These gristly, jaw-aching cuts are given the name 'hockey sticks'. Otherwise known as mutton chops or 365s.

'You're destined to become a pot licker, Smoke!'

For the farm dog who never leaves the couch, let alone the house. Smoke will also be accused of being a 'powder puff' or a 'Sunday dog'. The canine equivalent of a dole bludger.

'I'll have your guts for garters!'

Legend has it that serial killers of the early 1800s would use the guts from their victims to make garters, which would then be sold at market stalls. (Mental note for cows: Don't piss off Serial Killer Farmer Guy.)

'He's gained the bottom wire of the fence!'

The above refers to marrying the farmer's daughter, probably because it's the easiest part of the fence to make, as in: 'You shouldn't have too much trouble hooking up with her.' Though I don't know how the 'bottom wire of the fence' would feel about that!

'We need a new billy boy. Justin's as useless as tits on a bull.'

There's always a new kid in school. On the farm they're known as lambs, ewe lambs, gate-openers, remittance men or, as above, billy boys.

'He's had another brain fart.'

Refers to dogs, cattle and sheep who suddenly forget why they're on planet Earth, with unpredictable results.

'Just going to milk the girls over the backblocks.'

'Backblocks' is also used by Australians in reference to 'the back of beyond' and is often simply known in New Zealand as 'the bush'. The 'girls' are the four-legged, uddered variety.

'Hold your horses!'

Literally translated, this means to keep your horse still. Slow things down, take your time. For example: 'Hold your horses, Gaz, you only just met her on the internet, and now you want to marry her!'

'What are ya? A Queen Street farmer?'

Hailing from the big smoke, the Queen Street farmer is the city businessman who, upon encountering a midlife crisis, decides to buy some rural property. It's fair to say he's not the most practical fella on the farm. He doesn't favour getting his shoes dirty or getting up before 9am. After all, he didn't move to the farm to work!

'Must be from north of the Bombays!'

Also affectionately known as 'Dorkland', New Zealand's biggest city (just north of the Bombay Hills) gets a bad rap for being big. It happens everywhere around the world, mostly because we hate to see our big brother get too big for his boots.

'He's been in the herringbone since sparrow's fart.'

The herringbone shed is so-named because of the angle on which the (soon to be milked) cows are lined up. 'Sparrow's fart', as we've learned, means you should still be in bed.

SCHOOL
SPEAK

While it's true bottle flips have trumped marbles and slime has gazumped hopscotch, little else has changed in the Kiwi schoolyard. Kids still scrounge for shrapnel to buy steak and cheese pies and fights start over a box of Jaffas. There are, however, new phrases for the 21st century. The following will make you fit right in.

'I'll verse you at handball.'

For some reason, kids nowadays 'verse' each other, instead of 'play against' or 'challenge'. Sure, it's not the Queen's English, but then nor is 'C U L8R OR 2MRW 4 A SK8!'

'Last one in's a sissy!'

You can 'belly flop' or 'bomb' — just don't be the last one in! And no running around the pool!

'That is so random!'

A modern-day equivalent of 'that's so left field'.

'Tahi, rua, toru, wha!'

Without exception, every song sung by a primary school teacher on guitar starts
with these four words. It's Maori for 'one, two, three, four', if you've been living
under a rock. Or if you're from Hawera. I can say that — I was born there.

'Tin a cocoa, tin a cocoa, cuppa Milo.'

Honky (Pakeha) version of the Maori welcome: 'Tena
koutou, tena koutou, tena koutou, katoa.'

'Waipu? Cos you have to!'

Some New Zealand place names were surely written for kids. Juveniles — okay,
most of my mates — still laugh every time they drive past Waitomo.

'Why can I live in Otaki?'

Purely coincidental that three neighbouring towns in the lower North Island, when said together, comprise a completely rational sentence: 'Waikanae Levin Otaki!'

'What do you get when you cross a cow, a sheep and a goat?'

'The Milky Baaa Kid!'

'A . . . B . . . C . . . D . . . E . . . F . . . G! Ha, ha, you have to marry Gary!'

Remember eating an apple as a kid? You twisted the stalk round and round and whatever letter you landed on, that's who you would marry? It never worked, of course. If you hated Gary, for example, you'd just give it a good yank on 'F'.

'Ah . . . ear . . . e . . . or . . . oo!'

The sound of 30 Kiwi schoolkids learning vowels in Maori.

'What did God say when he ate Fiji?'

'I want Samoa.'

'I know you are, you said you are, but what am I?'

Some things never change.

103

'Why don't you marry it then?'

Hard to fathom, I know, but I still use this corker, as in: 'I love the 'Naki.' 'Why don't you marry it then?' Sure, you get a look of disbelief — as in, 'Grow up!' — but trust me, it's worth it. Especially if there are kids around.

'Nine girls are running under a wharf and here I am.'

The Kiwi version of 'A red Indian thought he might eat toffee in church'. The first letters of which spell 'arithmetic'. Similarly, the above is an easy way to remember how to spell 'Ngaruawahia'.

'Wainuiomata where the girls are smarter. Paekakariki where the boys are cheeky.'

One for the Wellington kids.

'Far out, say it, don't spray it!'

Some kids get a little excited when they speak, often showering the recipient with half the Waikato River. If the above doesn't work, try 'I want the news, not the weather'. If that doesn't work, do what every 21st-century family does: correspond only by text.

'Got any chuddy?'

Kiwi Speak for chewing gum.

'Giz a squiz at your answers.'

Cheating, Kiwi-style.

'Scrap! Scrap! Scrap!'

All good things must come to an end. The above, for example, is typically followed by the inevitable, slightly panicked squeal: 'Teacher's coming, teacher's coming!'

OLD-
SCHOOL
SPEAK

Take a deep breath — this may make you feel ancient. If you think Nomads, Treks and rat's tails still feature in School Speak, you'd better take your tube skirt and leg warmers back to 1985. That's more than 30 years ago!

Go on, admit it, you don't even know what a Year Six is. (It's Standard 4, ya manus!) Or what NCEA stands for. But let's move on. (It's 'National Certificate of Educational Achievement', in case you need it for Trivial Pursuit.)

'Here come the turds!'

Whoever coined this term, purely because it rhymed with
'third' former, deserves a cold Mello Yello.

'Wanna go round with me?'

Relationships were a lot simpler at primary school. Married to Daniel Smithson by morning tea, divorced by woodwork, and dating Joshua Ryan by lunchtime. 'Wanna go round with me?' was the junior equivalent of 'Can I buy you a drink?'

'Oh man, check out how many tags she's got on her Nomads!'

In later life — when you become a manager — status is determined by how many keys you have hanging from your belt, or where your name features on the in-and-out whiteboard at reception. At school, the coolest guy always had at least 28 tags on his Nomads. Mystery and intrigue surrounded this pigeon-toed god: How did he get them? Who did he beat up to get them? Only flags on your Chopper held more currency.

'Orrgh, ace buzz!'

Clocking the spacies game in the fish and chip shop in da '80s, ow!

'O curry curry arna, I found a squashed banana!'

A parody of New Zealand's unofficial national anthem, 'Pokarekare Ana'. Well known to New Zealand schoolchildren.

'Got a spare 20c for spacies?'

Before Xbox, PlayStation and Game Boy, there was Space Invaders in the fish and chip shop. It was the size of a jukebox, with greasy joysticks. Kids from all over would ask the above (of just about anyone) if it meant they could 'clock it' before their pineapple fritters arrived.

'Oma rapeti, oma rapeti, oma, oma, oma!'

Direct translation: 'Run rabbit, run rabbit, run, run, run!'

'One day a taniwha
Went swimming in the moana
He whispered
in my taringa
Won't you come
along with me
There's such a lot to see
Underneath the
deep blue sea.'

In Maori mythology, taniwha are formidable creatures that live in deep pools in rivers, dark caves or the sea. Friendly creature, then, to sing about at school.

'Cross-country tomorrow — are you gonna wag?'

Let's face it — cross-country and orienteering were built for madmen. At school, anyone who didn't cheat — or nip home for lunch at the halfway mark — was considered a freak. Wagging (Kiwi Speak for skipping school) may have been a sounder option.

'Can I borrow some Twink? I've got black Vivid everywhere.'

The rest of the world calls it Wite-Out; we call it Twink.
The rest of the world calls them markers; we call them 'Vivids'.

'She's such a mole!'

All these years we had it wrong. It was never 'mole,' but rather moll, which derives from the word molly, used as a euphemism for whore or prostitute. Weren't we charming?

'Grouse, who gave you the hickey?!'

When Shazza from third form came in with a golf-ball-sized rash on her neck, the rest of the class knew it wasn't from extreme vacuuming. Proof being that Shane Butler was smiling like a loon during 'sustained silent reading'.

'Mr Goston's banned Bull Rush!'

Known in Britain as Bulldog, Bull Rush wasn't a game for the slow or weak. Indeed, it was a lunchtime activity characterised by its high level of violence and physicality. This is probably why it was banned. But hell we had a good time!

'Silent but violent, loud and proud!'

School, unlike the workplace, was the ideal place to make everybody aware of your bodily functions. Sigh. Why do we have to grow up?

'She's a minger.'

She would scare a bulldog off a meat truck. Face like a dropped pie. Whichever way you look at it, the student in question isn't exactly an oil painting. Only a 'mole' is worse.

'Cabbage Maths.'

The direct opposite of Distinction with Honours, Cabbage Maths was a class designed for those who weren't exactly top of the heap. 'Cabbage' was also a handy putdown when one struggled for a more intelligent jibe. It also meant 'pot', which might be the very reason you ended up in Cabbage Maths. Ah, the circle of life . . .

'Hamu.'

Pronounced ha-moo, this term means to 'scab' or 'scrounge', though the direct translation is 'desperate'. Can be used when you've just bought a bag of chips and your excitable mates hear the rustle of the bag and swoop in like seagulls at smoko. Such 'mates' can afford their own chips, it's just that yours look more enticing. Plus they're free.

SKUXX
SPEAK

Skuxx Speak celebrates those hard-out terms used among the soon-to-be leaders of our nation. If you're gonna say them, make sure you slay them. Keen?

'Skuxx.'

You know the guy. He's the man, looks the part, has all the hook-ups. Occasionally the word deluxe (often spelt 'deluxx') is added after for extra effect.

'Chur.'

Even though Chur is a city in Switzerland, Kiwis use it as a strong voicing of thanks or agreement. 'Wanna bowl round to mine for the ABs?' 'Chur, cuz!' (cousin). Hit me up, chur.

'Egg.'

This classic term found fame in Aotearoa in the '80s and is widely used today, as of late largely thanks to Taika Waititi's homegrown movies. Use it when you can't think of a derogatory word for someone who has backed into your Holden, spilt a Hawke's Bay syrah on your cow onesie, or when Sonny Bill drops the ball right on the tryline.

'Spoon.'

See 'Egg'.

'Shot, bro!'

Can be used in response to many things: you finally got a girlfriend, got a record deal, ate all your vegetables, or got a phone call from All Blacks coach Steve Hansen.

'Lit.'

Back in the day, 'lit' meant to be so pleasantly drunk or stoned all the person could do was smile and look 'lit up like a light'. Interesting, then, that it is often used by the author's teetotal 11-year-old daughter. Thankfully, during school hours it also means 'awesome' or 'wicked'.

'Hungus.'

Refers to the first to arrive at, and last to leave, the hotel buffet. 'Hey, ow, stop being a hungus!'

'Manus.'

'Ya manus, you didn't put your togs and jandals in the boot! Well, no worries, she'll be right — we'll just mish down to the bach after some kai with the whanau.'

Note: Not to be confused with the following.

'Manu.'

The standard bomb requires the jumper to curl up into a ball and enter the water feet-first. The manu is when you hold the V-shape and your tailbone, or lower back, enters the water first. It's sick, bro.

'4 Realz?'

A likely reply when your friend says they very much enjoyed their large serving of mountain oysters (beef testicles).

'Cool story, bro.'

The ultimate in Kiwi sarcasm. Translation: 'That's all you've got?'

'Suss.'

As in 'suspicious'. 'He looks a bit suss' or 'That sounds a bit suss'. Possible scenario: 'Sorry, I can't come out. Tonight's the two-hour special of *Country Calendar*.' 'That sounds a bit suss.'

'Hard!'

'TJ's ugly, you reckon?' 'Yeah, hard.'

'Arks.'

'You better arks somebody!' 'Don't arks, you don't get.'
(Not to be confused with Noah's arks.)

'Mean, bro, mean!'

Your great-grandpa probably called it 'tip-top'. These days 'mean' translates
to 'wicked' or 'mint', as in: 'Two snapper on the same line, *mean*!'

'Straight up?'

As in: 'Are you being straight up? Are you telling the truth?'

'Wanna crash here?'

Sometimes a long lunch turns into a boozy dinner turns into thinking the wardrobe
doubles as a loo. Save crashing your car by crashing at your mate's house.

'Whack City.'

Should you be talented enough to be Queen or King of Whack City, you're in an elite
class of rugby or touch players. You can hot-step or side-step the best of them.

'Oh, *winner*.'

Despite its congratulatory connotations, being called a winner in New Zealand
typically means you have *lost* something: the match in the last second,
your keys down a drain, or your EFTPOS card when it's your round.

'Not even.'

Typical response to, for example, the suggestion of another nationwide flag referendum.

SATURDAY SPORTS SPEAK

Most Kiwi parents have one memory of Saturday mornings: driving their rug-rats from netball games to rugby games to cricket matches. Then, in the middle of the week, from netball practice to rugby practice to cricket practice. This ritual is as Kiwi as shark 'n' tatties on a Friday night. It's not uncommon for Chief Driver to All Events to quickly become Head Coach, Chief Washer of Filthy Socks and Shouter of McD's should their team win.

Sadly, the sideline is often littered with parents who, despite their best intentions and obvious talent, never became All Blacks and Silver Ferns.

Speaking of which, it should be said that New Zealand's obsession with rugby is matched only by its dogged determination to put 'all', 'black' or 'silver' into every national team nickname. For example:

All Blacks (rugby)	**Black Caps (cricket)**
All Whites (soccer)	**Tall Blacks (basketball)**
Silver Ferns (netball)	**Black Sox (softball)**
Black Ferns (rugby)	**Black Magic (America's Cup boat)**
Black Sticks (hockey)	**Black Beauty (A1 race car)**

This parochial naming of teams got a little out of hand a few years back when the New Zealand badminton team wanted to name themselves the, wait for it, Black Cocks. Certainly got the attention of those who thought the sport was boring. Anyway, I digress — back to the parents on the sideline . . .

'Oh, get off her!'

On the netball court, the player who is stuck to her opponent and
won't leave her alone is a prime target for this shout. Could be
followed up with: 'If she had a saddle, you could ride her!'

'Joshua, get onside!'

'Steven, you're all over the show!'

'Terence, don't dance with him, tackle him!'

'Jack, stick it up yer jumper and run!'

'Smash 'em into Tuesday, Stephanie!'

The ref at Saturday morning sport doesn't get paid — but does get abuse. These are a few you shouldn't use from the sideline:

'Wakey, wakey, touch judge!'

'I'm blind, I'm deaf, I wanna be a ref!'

'Move around, ref, that patch of grass hasn't seen the sun for 20 minutes!'

'Do you want a harmonica instead of that whistle, ref?'

'Come on, ref, are your eyes painted on?'

'I pee straighter than that, ref!'

'If that's 10 metres, ref, I would like you to fit me a carpet!'

Alas, when the kids leave the pitch and the big boys take over the real fun starts:

'Show 'im a clean pair of heels!'

'You couldn't pass wind!'

'You couldn't pass a kidney stone!'

'Run it like you stole it!'

'Your mum rang to say your bath is ready!'

'You couldn't score in a brothel!'

'Bring out the screens!'

In the old days, when a racehorse broke its leg on the track the owner would bring out a big screen, behind which the horse would be put down. Rugby fans have adopted it and will yell this out when their least-favourite player goes down.

HORSE-
RACING
SPEAK

Rugby, racing and beer — a recipe for Kiwi leisure. With its temperate climate, rich pastures and plentiful sunshine, Aotearoa has always been a pretty good place to jump on a horse. Race meets became a feature of the first anniversary celebrations in Wellington, Auckland, Nelson, Otago and Canterbury. The first ones were probably held around 1840 by the military garrison at Auckland.

Fast-forward about 180 years and there are a few things you need to know before you head down to the track: remember to load your pockets with dosh, wear a poncy hat (and that goes for the ladies too), and have a flutter on the trifecta, quinella, superfecta or exacta! Just be sure to read the following before you make a foal of yourself.

Poor puns aside, here's some jargon to get you through the Saturday meet.

'Bet until your nose bleeds.'

In racing terms, it's a 'dead cert' and punters should keep betting unless they become physically incapacitated.

'She's paying big bikkies.'

Super Wines, Gingernuts and Mallowpuffs are the biscuits of choice
in New Zealand. The bikkies for offer at the racetrack, however, will
go a lot further than what you dunk in your morning cuppa.

'Trust me to pick a chaff burner.'

Some people, me included, never win the meat pack down at the pub. Similarly, if I was to back a horse, I'd probably pick the one slower than a week of Sundays.

'Have a yarn to the asparagus.'

At the track, it's best to stick with the bloke who's done his homework. In horse-racing terms, that fount of knowledge resembles the spear-headed vegetable, as in 'more tips than a tin of asparagus'.

'You know what Stan's like; cuts his own hair.'

In the pub, he's the Scotsman. At the track, he's the punter who is extremely tight with his hard-earned coin.

'Trots on Sunday?'

Rest assured, this is not to suggest you may be spending your well-earned day off on the big white throne. In New Zealand, the 'trots' refers to harness racing.

'Here comes Cyril, he's such a bloody emu.'

Like a bum rummaging through bins for a meal, the 'emu' is the person who picks up discarded betting tickets on a racecourse, hoping that some will pay for his taxi ride home. This opportunist closely resembles Australia's largest native bird when feeding.

'They're getting up without names today.'

It's always a good day when the underdog wins. Indeed, that's probably why we follow sport. You'll hear the above at the course if a number of long shots have achieved the impossible.

'It'll pay the grandstand.'

Likely to be muttered when one or more outsiders wins or runs a place. The punter in question, unable to believe his luck, will no doubt follow the above quote with 'The Milky Bars are on me!'

'Better call the TAB, boy.'

Not many punters call it the Totalisator Agency Board, but a lot of Kiwis do call it!

'I wouldn't back it with bad money.'

Keep those mitts in your pockets. Or go and get another bag of chips.

'One Easybet thanks, mate.'

Some Kiwis throw their money at the pokies. Others like a scratchie
at the dairy. An Easybet is when you fling your loose change over
and let the one-sided, conniving computer pick your fate.

'Lucky I backed a mudlark!'

You have to know your horses, but you also have to know the conditions.
The above refers to the bolter that goes well on a wet track.

PUB
SPEAK

Ah, the Kiwi pub. The Patea Maori Club on the jukebox and cold Speight's on tap. The sound of the perfect pool break and girls dancing around their handbags. You'll hear the following lingo from the dartboard to the dunny.

'Maaaaaate!'

Many uses:

1. Hello.

2. Gidday.

3. Must be your shout.

'Are you unders or overs?'

No pub in New Zealand is complete without a pool table. Overseas, the balls are known as 'stripes and solids'. Here they're 'unders and overs'. And, whatever you do, don't sink the black off the break.

'Skull! Skull! Skull!'

The above is normally yelled during the heinous act of consuming
(on your 21st) what is commonly referred to as a 'yardy'. 'Skull'
is probably a variation of 'skol', a Scandinavian toast.

'How about a Waitakere Daiquiri?'

In West Auckland, where the footwear of choice is ugg boots (sheepskin boots) and family fights are started if someone from a Holden family buys a Ford, the Waitakere Daiquiri (bourbon and Coke) is a popular mid-morning beverage.

'Eating's cheating!'

A saying no doubt responsible for New Zealand's binge-drinking epidemic. Sadly, when you're in your late teens there's no such thing as good food and good wine. In fact, quite the opposite: a good chuck makes room for more beer.

'You got gorse in your pocket?'

Also dubbed the 'Aussie haka'. The bloke who never shouts, always heading to the bog when it's his round. 'Got katipos in your pockets?' can also be used.

'Can you believe this place hasn't got EFTPOS?'

Everyone remembers their flatting days, when being 'declined' was a common occurrence. Normally, it must be said, it was when you'd just ordered three rounds of tequila, a couple of chasers and five packs of salt and vinegar chips. For the most part, electronic funds transfer at point of sale is a great invention, although a little dangerous if you have a tendency to always shout the lads.

'Got any moolah for ciggies?'

'You got any spare pingas for fags?' works just as well. Or you could just spend your beer money on nicotine patches.

'If the mobile boxing doesn't finish soon, my Mrs will be ropeable.'

Translation: 'If the rugby league doesn't finish soon
my wife will have a noose ready for me.'

'Don't break the seal, bro.'

The fine art of holding off going to the loo as long as possible.
The theory is that once you start, you won't stop.

'Going to the footy this weekend?'

Use the word 'soccer' in the UK and prepare for the backlash. Americans call it soccer, Kiwis call it soccer, Brits call it football. But New Zealanders also call touch, rugby, league, and even soccer itself, footy or football. Confused?

'Wank you very crutch.'

Another annoying one from those people who can't help saying, 'Step into my orifice.'

'My round. You get the first one at the Cake Tin.'

Very shifty move by the buyer. Drinks at Wellington's stadium — known as the Cake Tin due to its distinctive shape — will cost an arm and a leg.

'Root.'

Fornicate. Go all the way. Bonk. Horizontal haka. You've heard about the national bird, right? Eats, roots, shoots and leaves?

'Far-kin-ell!'

Three innocent syllables heard across this fine nation from dawn till dusk. Often preceded by 'Shit-vers' or 'Farrr-*out*!'

Note: Should the perpetrator be in church or a school library, 'Kin-ell' will suffice.

'Got any electric puha?'

Otherwise known as 'dak', 'Bob Marleys' or 'Northland ciggies'. Whatever the name, expect to be asked to detour via Burger King on the way home.

'FMBs at two o'clock.'

Some people have a way with words. Whoever came up with 'f*** me boots' surely deserves some sort of literary award. Or a book voucher, at least.

'Chunder Mile.'

Oxford and Cambridge have a boat race; New Zealand universities once had an event which required participants to run a lap, eat a cold pie, skull a jug of beer and continue 'running' until they could no longer hold any of it in. Despite producing a raft of elite athletes, this practice has been largely banned by university authorities.

'Gizz us a hoon on your durrie!'

Meaning 'May I have a quick drag of your cigarette, kind sir?' Such a term can be extended, such as: 'OMG I could hoon an ice cream right now.'

'Piss.'

In New Zealand booze is otherwise known as 'piss'. You can get pissed, get on the piss, sink piss, take a piss, take *the* piss, or be as weak as piss.

Note: When in a bar on the piss you might also get pissy about a piss pour which is, for want of a better term, piss poor.

'Bugger.'

As versatile as the above. In New Zealand you can bugger things up, bugger off, bugger I've stubbed my toe, he's a dodgy bugger, she's a good bugger, bugger me I'm buggered. Ironically, the actual meaning of this word should never be googled.

'Hundy.'

As in a hundred bucks or 'pingas'. 'Hey, bro, I'll give you a hundy if I can crack two eggs on your head.' When they say, 'Deal', go ahead and crack just the one and leave. Kinda quick. 'Never said anything about *one*!'

'Piker, he's having an L&P!'

The drink Lemon & Paeroa, world famous in New Zealand, is fine with a splash of Southern Comfort. But if you get caught drinking it straight — and the rest of your mates have spent the evening working on a hangover of Jonah Lomu proportions — look out!

'Chilly bin.'

Known as an 'esky' in Australia, this portable ice chest can be used as a
seat, cricket stumps, or even a motorised vehicle should you feel like getting
arrested. Be sure you get the Kiwi pronunciation right: *chully bun*. Good.

'Where's the nearest
tinny house?'

Some Kiwis have very green thumbs and get hangry more often than the average
greenhouse attendant. They also speak another language entirely, using words like
dope, electric puha, 50, O and, lastly, cabb, which those in the know, know.

'Would you like to
leave a tip?'

Meaning unknown in New Zealand.

'You'd think he'd give us mate's rates.'

Not much point having a friend behind the bar if he doesn't pass on his staff discount.

'What do you want to go and live with those sheep stealers for?'

Former Prime Minister Rob Muldoon once said that New Zealanders who immigrate to Australia 'raise the IQ of both countries'. Still, if a Kiwi really wants to go and live with a bunch of sheep rustlers there's not a lot you can do.

'He's on his OE, earning big bikkies in London now.'

The big OE, or 'overseas experience', as it is commonly known, is a ritual for many Kiwis. Typically, it involves visiting 23 European countries in 18 days but not leaving the bar in each one. It also involves earning £3 an hour (that's about $9) in a grotty East London pub, sleeping under the stairs in a Willesden Green flat and going to The Church to complain about how much the Tube costs. Sometimes, though, it must be said, 'big bikkies' can be made if the right job is found. Then the OE never ends and Mrs Birch from Matamata sees her son only every second Christmas.

'That sheila just gave me the evils. Guess we won't be bumping uglies tonight.'

Self-explanatory. Let's not go into gory details.

'Mutton dressed as lamb.'

Could there be a more apt Kiwi saying? As if you didn't know, it refers
to a middle-aged or elderly person trying to look younger.

'Typical scarfie —
always on the turps.'

Local nickname for Otago University students, due to the extreme cold of
the south. By God they can drink; some of them can even study.

'Best get on the Shicker Express.'

Back in the days of the six o'clock swill, when men from all over the country would guzzle as much beer as they could before closing time, the Shicker Express, as it was known, was the first train, tram or bus to leave. It was named as such because you were normally 'shickered' when you got on it! The word 'shicker' is actually an adaptation of the Yiddish 'shiker' — incidentally, the surname of one of my mates. Always wondered why he enjoyed a pint.

'You're taking me on a tiki tour.'

Directed at the taxi driver who thinks he can take the long way home just because it's the end of the night and you happen to be utterly plastered.

13

STROPPY
SPEAK

It takes a lot to make a Kiwi lose their rag. A loss by the All Blacks will do it. Or being accused of being Australian. Generally, though, most Kiwis don't do their na-na unless they really have to.

Some would also venture to say Kiwis never have an opinion. That may be because Kiwis don't like to rock the boat, or cause grief for the sake of it. And although the joke 'Why did the Canadian cross the road? To get to the middle' could also apply to Aotearoa, it would be unfair to claim Kiwis don't know how to start a fight when need be.

It's most surprising then, given that most Kiwis are placid, unflappable types, the number of ways in which Kiwis do lose their rag. The following are muttered and spluttered from dairies in Dannevirke to malls in Mangere.

'SHUDDUP!'

Inspired by the one and only *Footrot Flats* cartoon.
Why use two words when one does the job?
(RIP Murray Ball.)

'Get stuffed.'

Usual response by any Kiwi when it's suggested his
homeland is a seventh state of Australia.

'Give her the evils.'

That other chick is dancing with your boyfriend. She'll be given either
the 'stink eye' or 'the evils'. Both lead to nowhere good.

'Get out of it!'

When your mate is about to take the last Snifter from the box. (RIP Snifters, sniff . . .)

'Bully for you.'

Typically muttered to a Kiwi workmate who has just received a pay rise, car park and free
trip to Rarotonga. Tall Poppy Syndrome at its finest. 'Whoopdee shit' also works just fine.

'Blimmin 'eck!'

A Kiwi's reaction to getting five numbers in Lotto.

'Blow me down!'

Same Kiwi getting six numbers.

'Spare me days!'

Realising it was last week's ticket.

'Bite your bum!'

Consider this a personal dedication to my Nana Noeline, who always used to say this. It's not surprising given that her younger sister, Margie, used to curse 'Poopy fart shit!'

'Don't get toey.'

In Aussie slang, 'toey' means 'sexually aroused'. The same word in
New Zealand means 'agitated' or 'annoyed'. The image originated
with horses on alert, toeing the ground with a hoof.

(Note: Whether they were slightly annoyed — or sexually excited — is still unclear.)

'Sorry, mate, you're shit out of luck.'

Muttered at barbies by the person who's secured the last coldie from the chully bun.

'Don't throw a hissy fit!'

Said to the Kiwi wife who's just been informed by her husband that he'd rather clean
the toilet than stay another week with the rellies. Also known as a 'wobbly'.

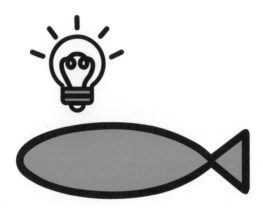

'Geez Wayne, you've got the brains of a chocolate fish!'

What a Kiwi says to his mate upon discovering he's running for Kim Dotcom's Internet Party.

'Keep yer shirt on!'

'Get off the grass!'

'Oh, bull pucky!'

'Bloody drongo.'

'You wouldn't know
shit from clay!'

'No need to spit the dummy.'

'You've got the brains of
a demented whitebait!'

'You couldn't organise a
piss-up in a brewery.'

'Don't have an epi.'

'You're all plaque, bay.'

'I'd spa him.'

'Sweet as, Arnkle.'

'Hey bay, what are
youse up to?'

'Wanna hiding, bro?'

ROAD-RAGE SPEAK

Kiwi drivers are among the worst in the world. Think, if you will, of that classic Disney skit in which Goofy — laid-back, warm, friendly, couldn't-do-enough-for-you Goofy — gets behind the wheel and instantly transforms into a homicidal maniac.

Kiwis don't know the meaning of 'merge'. They consider you a sissy if you let someone (anyone!) pass. And they have a colourful repertoire of sayings especially reserved for the confines of the Corolla.

'Did you get a horn for Christmas?'

Shouted at a driver with a lead hand.

'Do you think you own the road?'

A classic.

'Indicate, you loser!'

Some Kiwis don't turn their indicators off. Some don't even know they exist. Yell this at the driver who thinks we're mind-readers.

'Where'd you get your licence — a Weet-Bix packet?'

Most Kiwis remember, as kids, fishing around in the Weet-Bix packet for the latest promotional toy. But kids aren't dumb. Indeed, most throw their grubby mitts straight to the treasure and feed the remainder of the contents to the dog. The above is often yelled at a driver who clearly hasn't gained his licence the traditional way.

'Drive it or sell it!'

Muttered to the rich ponce in the Merc who doesn't know his clutch from his accelerator.

'Dunger.'

Your first car — a bomb, a rust bucket, and one in which it'll be impossible to 'fang it' to the gassy or servo (petrol station).

'Check out the drongo in the Mazda-bator.'

There was a time in New Zealand when every car had to be a Ford or a Holden. Somewhere along the way, the cheaper, sportier Japanese imports arrived. They were flashy, showy and seemed to be made of tin, and the above is an example of what your average V8 fan thought of them.

'Come on, it's not getting any greener!'

Bellowed at the driver who is lighting a ciggie, texting his mates and shaving when he's supposed to be moving forward. To make matters worse, this driver will panic and stall when he finally realises the lights have changed.

'It's in good nick — got a WOF last month.'

By no means is this an indication that the car in question comes with its own canine. WOF is short for Warrant of Fitness. Every car needs one; that's not to say every car has one.

'It's just a small ding.'

What the 16-year-old says to the car's owner when he hits the pine tree in the driveway.

'What a rust bucket! That old bomb shouldn't even be on the road!'

This car hasn't seen a WOF in years.

'You can take it for a blat, just don't prang it.'

The dictionary definition of 'blat' is 'to make a loud or raucous noise'. In this case, however, 'blat' means taking the car in question for a spin. And 'don't prang it' means: 'If you're going to take it for a test drive, don't hit the pine tree in the driveway.'

STREET
SPEAK

'Crash hot!'

'For real?'

'Primo!'

'What's the happs?'

'Too much!'

'That's sick!'

'Oh, true?'

'It's going off!'

'Oh, stink, bro!'

'You've had a mare!'

'Choice!'

'Sup?'

'Chur.'

'How many were there?' 'Untold.'

'Statue, bro?'

Correct answer to: 'What did one Maori statue say to the other Maori statue?'
More commonly used when two people meet on a pitch-black night.

'Bruce's moved from A-von-da-lay to Papa-two-toes.'

Just as Hyacinth Bucket on *Keeping Up Appearances* preferred to be known as Hyacinth 'Bouquet', so too do folk in Avondale and Papatoetoe prefer a more upmarket pronunciation of their suburbs' names.

'It was mint! I got it from the Ware Whare.'

Getting a bargain at The Warehouse.

THINGS
YOU'LL
NEVER HEAR
A SELF-
RESPECTING
KIWI MALE
SAY

'Let's think big.'

'I don't mind if Australia wins this one.'

'Russell Coutts is still a full-blooded Kiwi in my books.'

'I'll have a shandy.'

'Let me tell you how to get to my favourite fishing spot.'

'We're heading to Invercargill for the summer.'

'Do you like my Stubbies? I got them from Hallensteins.'

'Make mine a Rheineck.'

'I won't have a pie — bad for the blood pressure.'

'I'll just have an instant.'

'I'll have another piece of quiche.'

'I should finish *The Luminaries* by the weekend.'

'I totally understand NCEA.'

'We need someone like Muldoon in charge again.'

'I think I'll do some study instead of playing touch tonight.'

'MMP is really clear cut.'

'I'm going to hire someone to mow my lawns.'

'We forgive the French.'

Acknowledgements

Firstly, I want to thank anyone who has bought this little book since it began life ten years ago.

Since then NZ has added some classic lingo, but we've also lost a few good mates. In particular, I want to thank Murray Ball and John Clarke, who shaped our country with their words and ideas.

Chur to those who offered sayings and memories of Aotearoa. Big ups to my folks, Chris and Lyn, who gave me no end of material for the parental chapters. And thanks for laughing at my jokes, sis.

Much aroha to my wife, Amy, and my two girls, Sophie and Georgia.

Sweet as!

Justin Brown
March 2018
www.justinbrownbooks.com